W. S. Graham was born in Greenock in 1918. His first book of poems, *Cage Without Grievance*, was published in 1942. Subsequent volumes were *The Seven Journeys* (1944), *2nd Poems* (1945), *The White Threshold* (1949), *The Nightfishing* (1955), *Malcolm Mooney's Land* (1970) and *Implements in Their Places* (1977). His *Collected Poems 1942–1977* appeared in 1979. He lived his last years in Cornwall, and died there in 1986.

by the same author

COLLECTED POEMS
1942–1977

W. S. GRAHAM
Aimed at Nobody
Poems
from Notebooks

edited by

MARGARET BLACKWOOD

and

ROBIN SKELTON

with a Foreword by

NESSIE GRAHAM

faber and faber

First published in 1993
by Faber and Faber Limited
3 Queen Square London WC1N 3AU

Photoset by Wilmaset Ltd, Wirral
Printed in England by Clays Ltd, St Ives plc

A CIP record of this book
is available from the British Library

ISBN 0–571–16745–4

1 3 5 7 9 10 8 6 4 2

Contents

Foreword

Due to a variety of circumstances, when Sydney was preparing his volume of *Collected Poems* a considerable number were omitted. However, time and again he said that he did not disown any of his poems. When commenting on his work, he remarked that every poem was relevant; that it was integrated into the whole body of his writing. Were it later to have been a question of choosing a book of Complete Poems, I know he would have included everything that he wrote and kept.

At various times it was suggested to Sydney that the poetry was progressing better. But no. He said repeatedly to different people that earlier poems were not necessarily less good than later ones.

I remember once joining him, helping to crumple up and throw on the fire a great number of drafts of poems. When I said, 'Are you sure about all these?', he replied reassuringly, 'Oh yes. I know what I'm doing.'

But the work of the notebooks survived his rigorous judgement and *Aimed at Nobody* affords an opportunity for 'somebody' (or 'nobody'!) to encounter it. For making this book, my thanks are due to the editors and in particular to Robin Skelton, who has long been a champion of W. S. Graham. Finally I wish to thank Margaret Snow, without whose help my part in this publication would not have been possible.

Nessie Graham

Introduction

The fragments here collected have been taken from notebooks and miscellaneous worksheets that W. S. Graham sent to me over a period of several years when, in an effort to prevent him destroying or losing material that I knew would be of great importance to followers of his work, and in order to augment his tiny income, I sent him a small monthly cheque. It was a time when he was in limbo as regards book publication. *The Nightfishing* had appeared in 1955, in the same year as my own first collection, and though both our books were well received, his being indeed applauded, the 'Movement' in British poetry began that same year with the publication of Philip Larkin's *The Less Deceived*, and the new fashion for understated ironic verse began to dominate the scene.

From 1955 to 1970 no new collection of poetry by W. S. Graham appeared, though he continued writing. When in the late sixties I asked Faber & Faber why they had not seen fit to bring out a new Graham book I was astonished to be told that they had lost touch with him and did not know he was still writing. I told them that indeed he was still writing and certainly had enough material for a new book. I had myself published a number of his poems in *The Malahat Review*, and others had appeared, over the years, in the *New Statesman*, *The Listener*, *The Cornish Review*, *Poetry* (Chicago) and *Botteghe Oscure*. I gave them Sydney's address and *Malcolm Mooney's Land* appeared in 1970, to be followed by *Implements in Their Places* in 1977 and a volume of *Collected Poems* in 1979.

The *Collected Poems* was, in reality, a rigorously edited 'selected poems'. It included none of the work from *The Seven Journeys* of 1944, and only eleven poems from *Cage Without*

Grievance. It was, indeed, Sydney's own choice of his canon, and he was more critical of his own work than any other poet I have ever met.

This being the case, it is clear that Sydney himself would have frowned at the publication of this book were it to be issued as anything other than a collection of work which he had either discarded or left incomplete, and it must be emphasized that these fragments are being published primarily because they shed light upon his other work, even though it is clear that many of them would have been judged brilliant by anyone other than their author.

Even though I say this, I must also say that Sydney did intend his notebook material to be seen by people interested in his work. This is clearly revealed in the poem ('Proem') written in Notebook 4 as a kind of preface, in which he says of the book that 'It is aimed at nobody at all' and adds that 'It is now left just as an object by me / to be encountered by somebody else.'

Encountering these notebooks, or fragments from them, here, one notices immediately that images, phrases and devices that appear in the official canon also appear in other incomplete poems. In 'The Dark Dialogues', for example, we read of 'the door / With the loud grain and the name / Unreadable in brass', and in the discarded 'Greenock Dialogues' we find the lines, 'The top-flat door, my father's name / Scrived by his own hand in brass.' In 'Clusters Travelling Out' we have the lines, 'I think I hear you hearing me. / I think I see you seeing me.' And in the notebooks we find the line, 'I hear you almost seeing me.'

The notebooks do not only give us a captivating glimpse into the poet's workshop, however. They also let us see what might be called his playground or, to use the North American expression, rumpus room. There are many doodles, many verbal games, some of them Joycean and some not, and there are numerous drawings. Some of these are of a woman's face in a style reminiscent of Picasso; some remind one of the work of his friends Robert Colqhoun and Robert MacBride. One notebook contains anatomical drawings and photographs, for it was originally a medical textbook; and these have been transformed by Sydney with ink and wash.

In endlessly fascinating letters Sydney commented on the poet's task and the poet's difficulties. He found communication with others a deep necessity, as well as a formidable problem. On 29 September 1970 he wrote to me, 'Write me a letter. Silence has no vocabulary to speak of.' Two years later, on 8 December 1972, he summed up in another letter to me a great deal about the making of poetry: 'What a mysterious, unsubstantial business it is, writing poetry. After one finishes a poem which seems to work one says Ha Ha now I'll write another because I know how to do it but it is not so. There is the silence before one just as difficult to disturb significantly as before. What one has learned is inadequate against the new silence presented.'

Here, then, are some of W. S. Graham's words to disturb the silence, and while he himself did not consider these disturbances significant, we are entitled to think otherwise.

Robin Skelton

EDITORIAL NOTE

The spelling in these poems has not been altered if it seemed idiosyncratically correct. Titles have been added where necessary (in square brackets). For source material and notes, see pages 65–68.

Margaret Blackwood

Proem

It does not matter who you are,
It does not matter who I am.

This book has not been purposely
made for any reason.

It has made itself by circumstances.
It is aimed at nobody at all.

It is now left just as an object by me
to be encountered by somebody else.

Notebook 4, *c.* 1973

The Ballad of Willie Peden

I

Draw your breath on this then
    And leave the dogs to bark
For you are fell upon this place
    And its tenses are dark.

II

Feather your ears on silence
    And watch what you're about
For you will have your say enough
    Before the night is out.

III

An act we shall be other to
    Runs on as the dogs bark.
Draw your breath on mine then
    And draw the little cork.

IV

And then the dark disclosed him
    And one wisp of light.
By the light of the glowires small
    Across the ground he went.

V

Whatever time this falls upon,
    Or distantly ago,

These voices that remurmur it
    Are not voices I know.

VI

And silence has disclosed him
    Another element
And he has set that bonny back
    To travel this event.

VII

He came to the quick water then,
    Went that water along.
The wee whistle his breath made
    Was like the finch's song.

VIII

And when he came to the Whin Hill
    And set him at the brae
The whistle in his breath was loud
    As you would blow a key.

IX

Draw the little cork for me
    For he is pressed sorely,
And he is caught in the right side.
    Can that disguise be me?

Worksheets (*The Nightfishing*), *c.* 1952

[The Circumstances Are Still Infinite]

1

Dear Alan, your Stockport-horned head's not here
Hung between the hart and the Wildebeest.
Zambesi heads and the head-waters of Welsh
Rivers are speaking for us both tonight.
Major Wynne tones in the Africa of his years
Knocks on the wall of darkness with a light.
The circumstances are still infinite.

2

Sit in a room of heads. The poems I've made
Are mad in my own lifetime hung for sport
On walls the grammarsow shall soon put down.
Put us into the yard together to talk.
The mind's a betting yard where bets are laid
On creatures we put up into the light.
The circumstances are still infinite.

3

The misty stars are sitting high tonight
In a rocking chair of hills and over Wales
My ear hovers to take a little part.
Stockport puts in its bit to what I write.
The circumstances are still infinite.

Notebook 3, *c.* 1970

Surrealgraphs

1

After the rain the delivery trucks
On East 22nd went dead to silence
And slowly somersaulted into
The mauve mist with nothing to tell.
And look they soared to almost nothing
But we can see they are spilling cargoes
Down on us. Watch your heads. They
Rapidly approach down through
The mauve and they are shouting
Watch your heads down there below
I fall down in the name of the people.
From the crashed cartons sprang
Bones and flesh and hair and became
One man tall and tenor. 'Justice
With courage is a thousand men.'

2

Maiou Maiou my little furry flower.
I hear you have been endangering vessels
Off the Mull of Kintyre. That's all I said
From lying in my bed to the flower
That grows out of the crack in the ceiling.
I went to sleep into the arms
Of the quick first dream but even
At that there I was in a saga

So much pulling at the oars that
The skin might often be seen left
Behind on the wood i.e. on the handle.
Maiou Maiou my little furry flower.

3

Where would you rather be? I do not know.
I have been put down in Crete.
I am in Heraklion standing beside
The sparking shops like square caves.
This is the street of the knife-temperers.
The street is crowded. My dreaming eyes
Are swept clean by moustaches.
No one looks at me because I am here
Only if I wear a devised beast's head.
This mask has curls of red ragworm.
The eyes are cut too wide apart.
My dead mother is sitting in a hive
Of sparks grinding blades and coughing
Sulphur and three men in the shop
Are at their treadles grinding edges
And plunging them into the green barrels.
O what fumes and my nostrils pinched.
Now the four of them are singing
Great moustached songs. Even my mother
Has a moustache. She seems happy.

Worksheets (unpublished poems), 11 November 1975

[One Good Sound]

One good sound is the sound of nature occurring
At the flayed edge of the idea's ear.
I think today I will fly away. I must
Not say that. I am in my own country
Enough for my own good. I want to stay.
And yet I am on the road hurrying away.

If you ever find me at large again under
The clouds flying like white postmen bearing
No folded messages, please nod your head
And grunt something which will be a sign.
Hurry and speak to me fast. I am being
Chased across the land shouting nothing.

And now the black conveyance drawn by violet
Horses draws up beside me walking to take
Me out of myself shyly wanting to go
Where within me a country has never been.
Good Morning. How do you do. Language
And I enter this eccentric carriage.

I know you cannot follow me but please
Try by example to travel even disguised
Across this part of the country even although
The season is not fashionable. O holidaymaker
On language and its environs, you are now
Entering country where only the words go.

I speed along the cambered rain-blue road
Being a flying translator translating
English into English. Chance particulars
Flow past my windows of fine water to fall
To travel forever back. You will observe
The love for their job my wind-screen wipers have.

Where we are going we can hardly see
From here. That hill to the right, that rusted bracken
Inclination of rogue fields and granite
Is lower Zennor Hill. The raven top
Is sailing blind above that in the mist.
We turn off here and up to the right. At least

This is not it. This is only the sound
Of nature occurring at the ear's flayed edge
Where idea begins and language starts
To want to go somewhere, to want to be
Alive in another animal in its particular
Antic. I have fallen down into a colour

Of calling out from rusted, red bracken
Across the loch to you. The morning breathes.
Do you think anybody hears? The sand pipes
Its bivalves into air. And I am read
Like plastic from a picknick on the shore
Keep in a cool place. Shake before you pour.

The point is this is not it and that
And that, those dear hastening particulars
Going past me looking in are not easily
My speaking friends of the day, they come from where
They naturally lurk to speak or not to speak.

Worksheets (unpublished poems), *c.* 1972

The Eighth Letter

When the word or the word's name
Falls out before us in winter,
Beware of the cunning god
Who crunches across the tense
Fields ready to pretend
To carry this letter between us.

This is the eighth letter
Abridged, of course. The frozen
Spittled messenger lurks
And prowls, anxious to be whistled
To heel to carry the message.
He is better over a distance.

Worksheets (unpublished poems), *c.* 1970

Pangur

Pangur, my cat (look) jumps,
Foreign to me, at the invisible
Mouse. He is back in my house
Where I am kept from by trying
To speak to you. And why have I
Been put into this ridiculous
Dream because I only wanted
To speak for once thoroughly
To another? Bring in the sea again.

I am not allowed the privilege
Of having Pangur here. At least
The mouse invisible I see.
I could entice it onto my knee
And let it speak for both of us.

Worksheets (unpublished poems), *c.* 1970

Myself the Day Desires

Myself the day desires I thought
So I woke early up and scrubbed
My parts and spirit and went out
As hero to see what I could find.

I walked across and I walked between
Black Madron's trees with my stick
Swishing the nettles of the queen
And I gave the young brambles an extra lick.

And over my desiring head
The morning sky was trailed by others.
So I was out by these words led
Between the hedges and the feathers.

If while I tell you this you want
To interrupt with your some question
Think twice. The dear I am infant
Has started out and he is gone

Is gone on the blue rainlit road
Away and away from what the words call
Anything that I never could
Have as my home at all.

Worksheets (unpublished poems), 26 October 1969

[To Find and Find]

Let me say we almost see ourselves
Across the half mile of the morning
Loch.   There is nobody else here.

Behind me in an eye saw down
Over the bracken from the high hazel
I am a man holding the restless
Stem of a skiff at the loch's edge.

I stand across from you with one
Foot in the loch and see across
The white speckle of your home farm
With all you do that I love in it.

Shall I come across? Can you put me off?
Why should I stand at the thirteenth line
On the loch's edge? It is a real loch
And stretches more than by Art made.

     I push out across
     The terrible shallows
     Across to see who is it
     I put my back into
     The oars to come across
     To see?   You will know.
     No one else will know,
     Who I am crossing
     This space to see.

I lean back on the blades and send
Two lines of whirlpools out over
The loch I go to find and find.

Worksheets (unpublished poems), *c.* 1970

[Kandinsky's Ribbons]

Remember it is necessary to be aware
Of every shape, of every kind of silence
That slides past the making ear. Curious
Visiting creatures, don't frighten them off. They are
Your medium from everywhere from even under
The towering pressures of the sea-trench where
The choir of urchins and the sea-stars sing
From their dark ledges and Kandinsky's ribbons
Of weed with yellow follicles lean with the moon.

Worksheets (*Malcolm Mooney's Land*), Folder A, *c.* 1967

[From the Sleeping House]

Look down from a height on the long
Oystercatching shore of Loch
Long at first light with the tide
Streaming out between the pools
And you will see. Don't breathe
Or frighten me waiting to meet
My dear from the sleeping house coming
Over the shingle with her bare feet.

Notebook 4, *c.* 1970

The Dredge

With you present I empty out
The deep-sea dredge. Is there any
Creature which interests you? You
Must watch your feet and put this down
In your life-book and begin

A new curiosity. On this deck
A knot of seaweeds and creatures
Squirms. Kandinsky's micro worms
Are still alive under the weed
To nose out at us two who read.

From the pressures in a kind of jelly
Bag I find I find some other
Lives not unlike what I think
My own life looks like. Your life
Is the red ragworm with the mouth

Gaping shouting why have you taken
Me into a difficult place to play
At what? There was one lost sea
Star clasped on nothing under the yellow
Follicled kelp would not let go.

With you present I sort out
The eatable from the deadly rare.
You have put aside with care
As precious bait to downward wind
Into the fathoms of your kind.

Worksheets (unpublished poems), 5 October 1971

[More Shots of Mister Simpson]

[1]

After the rain slewing light
Makes blue the pools between the bull
Rushes and very patient the subject
Stands in his geranium morning
Dressed in his navy-blue best
Outside his cottage in Nancledra.

He stands to be put down. He wants
Some pictures of himself to send
He says over to America.
So we are here, neither of us
For a fee. I see him looking in
At me as a minute passes. His face
Cascades across the eye of the world.
I have him.

That's it, Mister Simpson. You can relax.
But I think I took two faces.
Who was it looking from behind
The black window-glass shouting
With a white face of no sound
Out through the November me
To tell me that the camera
Or myself could not hear?

Ah Mister Simpson, Mister Me,
Standing under the flying blue
Sky-light of our November under
Zennor Hill, has anything at all
Been done? My cheap camera does not
Allow us nearer. One attempt
For the road and that is finished.

Reader, kestrel, Zennor Hill,
Nephews neices on the mantelpiece,
Unheard voice of master, Mister
Simpson I close up now and turn
Away to go home nearly home.

Worksheets (*Implements in Their Places*), Folder B, [1]
3 May 1971, [2] 16 July 1971

A Dream of Crete

And wakened into sleep to find
Myself diving with ancient speed
Out of newspaper news into
Sincerely yours slowing into
A slow dive descending lonely
Over Malia at night with words
Trailing like bubbles above me from
My slow body falling down
Into Papakouri's grove.

Mother, Mother, I am landing
Myself in an enormous word
Ship down on the silence of Crete.

    I have been here before.

Awake observe how underneath
His sleeping lids his eyes belong
To not one of his company.
Can we suppose by their movement
They are watching a place with people
Going to and fro, actual
People who stand and sit and prop
A goat stick in the corner and sit.

2

A dream of remembering between
Words in a crowded dark cave
Taverna and I can't hear any
Single person speak. I can't
See anybody I might know. I can't
Breathe in the bed O I am being
Floated out like a drowned man
Between the men between the buzzing
Instruments to a dark table.

Notebook 4, *c.* 1970

In Crete

It is always strange when some other
Voice comes in on the silence we think
Is natural to us, is our home.
I heard. I hear. I long to hear
The Greek owl say his say.

The cry astonished the jug I held
And pierced the room. A cold room
Filled with the January Cretan air.

The Cretan owl has made his voice
And attitude to his own place.
Pleepo pleep. Give me a stopper
To keep the water in to wash
My cheeks imprinted by the guilt
Of not being a peasant. Give
Me, Malamanopolis, another ouzo.

You see here I am lonely in another
Land. I am lonely in another
Full stop period. We are all
Moving or circling what we go around.

Worksheets (unpublished poems), *c.* 1969

[In the Street of Knives]

To make this scene in a certain fashion
This is how it is. I am sitting
In near darkness looking out from
Myself at foreign people trying
To peer through the dream of Art into
Their polite unbelieving eyes.
It is a Taverna in Malia in Crete.
An ordinary death has taken place.
Bread has been baked for the dead.
Grandfather Paroclasis enters
In the guise of a goat hero
To find Nana his daughter
Speaking to a foreigner
Swimming in the corner chair.
The terrible thing it is all
True and through the ouzo
Glass I can feel him fixing
Me straight. Then Skrates enters and
His Coca Cola son who has been
In the states. I see you three.
You will please allow me to look
At you and your olive daughter
And her husband who has no
Olives but has a mountain moustache.

Why I am here is not the point.
I am the recording tourist hero
Swimming down to stand to walk
In Heraklion in the street of knives.

I am beckoned into the dark
Cave of treadles grinding edges.
Sparks belonging to no time
Are falling down on the floor. Fumes
Of burnt metal enclose two boys
With forced moustaches. I show how later
I tempered steel on Clydeside
And sip Retsina and keep looking
For who it is my slow dive takes
Me down towards. My tourist eyes
See the donkeys with blue beads,
See bible trees in the square,
See a young widow hidden.

Notebook 4, *c.* 1972

[On the Other Side of Language]

Hitherto uncollected I proceed
As a shoal yet like iron filings
Made to beg to the magnet, I
Go in some almost-Victorian direction
Towards my fate, towards my fate.
O what, O what will become of us,
The heroine near to fainting cries.
I do not live in that book tonight
As the owl leaves the tree and takes
His fusilage in a few heavy
Slow flaps down to the little mouse.
The wood is quiet as I wander
Here on the other side of language.
Only a twig from the top floor
Seems to love another audibably.
Leave it. It is only the other
Wind trying to disturb
The formal barrier between
You and I, wherever you
Are listening from, opening up
Your personal package to eat a sandwich.

Here I go on the other side
Of language and the great age
Of language floors me, what an old
Barrier having to do with every-
Thing that has ever been worth
Anything, surrounds me and keeps me cosy,
Tight, or dead if you want that.

Hello. Hia. Are you there? Can you hear
Me through the deafening silence as
It waves over the high towering
Beeches? You are hearing everything
And that, Dear Sir, is your trouble.
What will you do? O do not ask
The poor man on the other side.
I am only trying to get home
And I mean that in my lifetime.
Please keep me from going quickly down
Into the manhole. It's not my style.
Give me a hoot like a red Indian
From the north-west edge of the trees.

Worksheets (unpublished poems), *c.* 1965

[Nature Is Never Journalistic]

Nature is never journalistic.
It does not tell us to tell how
It is faring now. We still go
All of us in our lanes and roads
Immersed in that which is not us.

In fact last Tuesday afternoon
I locked myself in my coat and closed
The door and threw myself on the mercy
Of rainy December, a new month.
One step two step three step more.

Four step five step I went falling
Into the outofdoors world
To give myself a shake to shake
The words I live on up a bit.
I see an old tin can in the hedge.

It is not speaking. Here I am
On Tuesday the   of December
At five o' clock walking the road
Between the whining, beaded hedges
For nothing nothing nothing nothing.

If you would like to contact me
Wait at the telephone pole whose top
Shows just over the misty brink
Of that next hill. Be sure you are
A woman with all a woman's best.

Now as the blinders whistle for dusk
And my simple sophisticated boots
Clip on the road as my metrenome
You should look out for me coming up
Soon to be seen from your side

Worksheets (unpublished poems), 11 December 1969

Fill In This Form

Your name in capitals. Birth place.
Your mother. Your father. Sex. What
Illnesses have you had. Scars.
Description. Fair. Dark. Height.
Weight. Feet. Member. Moles. Hair.
Is your nose long, short, broken, none?

Do you take after your father? Do you
Take after your mother? Do you take
After a monster somehow composed by
You from an idea of them both? Which
Parent gave you the best of you?

If you have only one parent alive
Which would you choose? If they are both
Dead do you think they would like you
As you are now filling in this form
In the private room. Was your father
Ever a member of the Communist Party?
Was he ever a vegetarian or helped
To fix the acoustics of the Albert Hall?

Have you ever been in any trouble?

Worksheets (unpublished poems), 5 May 1971

[I Am Told You Speak My Language]

Straighten your face. Stand still.
You will not smile or blink your eyes.
These questions I will ask, you you
Will not answer. I will answer.
You are not repeat not to speak.

I have never seen you before but
I know you because I know your kind.
Stand still. You are forbidden to speak.
Have a cigarette. Don't move.
Stop that. Stand still. No tears here.

What are you frightened for? I'm just
Another man. Attention. Stand straight.
Brothers and sisters, have you some?
Your lips wherever they come from must
Not move or quiver a fraction. Silence.

You realise you are keeping me late.
I am told you speak my language although
We are not from the same place. Stop
Making your hands to fists. Step
A pace forward and don't speak.

How did you get yourself into this
Position? Be a man, my boy,
Your mother maybe said. You realise
I am your friend maybe the best
One you will meet. Stand up straight.

Notebook 4, 23 October 1970

About the Stuff

O lens of language, how can I focus
My long-sea gun on the white paper
To brown and black and char and startle
It into a speaking flame? The leper
Medium should be black and rise
Into a dazzle bad for the eyes.

Who wants to set the whole hill-side
Bracken foxgloves and playing vixens
On fire? No, only it is I want
To disturb the paper, to burn a sense
Of a changed other person in
On to the white of this public skin.

I have put my ground lens in my pocket.
I did not mean to speak but just
To lie down hidden away on the hill
Above Zennor. But I think I must
Get up out of the humming hill
Side and go down for a conflagrating
Pint of the Tinner's cold ale.

Worksheets (unpublished poems), 30 August 1968

[This Little Evening]

Clawhammered face, hammerheaded
Land-shark of this little evening
Of drinks together afterwards,
I don't know how your almond-faced
Wife stands you for a second. Please
Can I freshen your drink? Yes I agree
Cows miss the intellectual impact
A real work has. Take Dianne there
She's more aware of you watching
Her being aware than aware of what
Friell is saying with those spaces.

You would like to take me outside?
I won't go. But maybe Dianne
And I will get our coats and leave
And walk through the dusk of the square
Tenderly and find a taxi
To take us to a place together.

Notebook 4, *c.* 1971

The Honey Game

Lightly the light. Let's try the Honey
Game you and I are best at.
Because I know you are broken
I can put you together again.

Round the house the afternoon
City in an overcoat of light
Swivels to look. I toss the coin.
Who is it shall begin?

So the window of their time
Turned to dusk and looked in.
Dusk being not you or me
Saw only a killed swan.

I see you also as a swan
Very unslain lying there.
Lightly the light, sweet the shame,
Us playing at the honey game.

Notebook 4, 5 August 1970

As Told to Davie Dunsmuir

Later when the whole thing had blown
Over I ran into her dressed
To kill or maim at least in one
Of the Late Nights at the Town Hall.

I didn't like the one she was with.
A good dancer though. She saw
Me too, sure enough. I saw
Her face before she put her smile

On and turned to him with her hand
Possessive on his padded shoulder
Ready for the last waltz. I thought
Well this is it, I'm out. And yet

When they played The Queen and I got my coat
She must have dumped him because
Well there she was on her own. I said
Can I walk you home? And then without

A word she took my arm and well
That was that, like old times,
Her leaning in on me, her heels
Clacking along in the small hours.

Worksheets (unpublished poems), 5 February 1966

Waiting for Snow

Waiting for snow I look out
At a few scattered rooks blown
Against the pewter sky. Who
Is Hasse? The voice from the deep
Freeze announces a flute concerto.

Waiting for snow I look out
At a few scattered rooks blown
Against the pewter sky, Jemima,
Hold me tight, hold me tight.
Damn you, damn you, Demetrius
Why have you come at this time?

Waiting for snow I look out
At a few scattered rooks blown
Against the pewter sky. Maybe
I should have asked some friends in
To wait. To wait for what?
                                    The slow
Cold November dusk grows
Out of Trevayler's waving woods.

Worksheets (unpublished poems), *c.* 1970

[The Particular Object]

The particular object must not nearly lose
Its name. In my dear dying light the name
Is —u—. Its hide I'll have and choose
The cured-by Art best areas on my frame.

So late at night I fall to find beside
Me on its side this object not moving.
Your name is —u— beside the Clyde
From which you sprung only Clydeside speaking.

—u—, you dear abstract object
Fastened below the waterline to the Old
Custom House Quay where my father, wrecked,
Took me on Sundays, I stood and stood and called

Down as a boy through the industrial, oily
Water to find you. —u—, please tell
Me now when neither of us can recognise me,
How you are. From here how shall I call?

Many a time at night I fall to find
You still under the water over the quay's
Edge half out of sleep. Then I pretend
To say your name to put us at our ease.

Maybe it is a pity to make you so dramatic.
You are not that at all. But did you hear me
When I called down from the quay-side to ask
Your name? My —u—. My —u—.

Worksheets (unpublished poems), 8 October 1971

[Malcolm Mooney's Figment]

Why I can be articulate and
Dream at the same time does not matter.
I have the licence. Greenock also
Has its deserved licence to speak
To me, its child, dreaming to meet it
Here late in the oily firth night.

Always when I stop saying hello
And lie down to sleep I know I have
A small dried up Greenock under my pillow.
Malcolm and what he stands for sips
His hurried last and as I pass
His silhouette shows through RAB NOOLAS.

What shall I do, me trying
To speak to Greenock like a person?
I know my infant, childhood, youth,
Sweet town not at all, only
I happen to be Malcolm Mooney's
Figment rocked on Malcolm's knees.

Notebook 4, *c.* 1968

The Greenock Dialogues

I

O Greenock, Greenock, I never will
Get back to you. But here I am,
The boy made good into a ghost
Which I will send along your streets
Tonight as the busy nightshifts
Hammer and spark their welding lights.

I pull this skiff I made myself
Across the almost midnight firth
Between Greenock and Kilkreggan.
My blades as they feather discard
The bright drops and the poor word
Which will always drown unheard.

Ah the little whirlpools go
Curling away for a moment back
Into my wake. Brigit. Cousin
Brigit Mooney, are you still there
On the Old Custom House shore?
You need not answer that, my dear.

And she is there with all the wisps
And murmers in their far disguise.
Brigit, help with the boat up
Up over the shingle to the high
Tide mark. You've hardly changed, only
A little through the word's eye.

Take my hand this new night
And we'll go up to Cartsburn Street.
My poor father frightened to go
Down the manhole might be in.
Burns' Mary sleeps fine in
Inverkip Street far from Afton.

And here's the close, Brigit. My mother
Did those stairs a thousand times.
The top-flat door, my father's name
Scrived by his own hand in brass.
We stand here scrived on the silence
Under the hissing stairhead gas.

II

I (Who shall I be?) call across
The shore-side where like iron filings
The beasts of the tide are taken through
Their slow whirls between the words.
Where are you now, dear half-cousin
Brigit with your sandprints filling
In the Western, oystercatching morning?

This is a real place as far
As I am concerned. Come down over
The high-tide bladder-wrack and step
Over the gunwale of our good skiff.
I lean back on the bright blades
To move us out on language over
The loch in the morning, iodine air.

Abstract beasts in a morning mirror
By memory teased very far
Out of their origins. Where where

[38]

Shall I take us as the little whirl
Pools leave the blade and die back?
The house is shrinking. Yeats' hazel
Wood writes in a dwindling style.

From where I pull and feather I see
You dearly pulled towards me yet
Not moving nearer as we both
Move out over the burnished loch.
Move with the boat and keep us trim.
If it is a love we have, then it
Is only making it now, Brigit.

III

I am not trying to hide
Anything anything anything.
My half-cousin Brigit
With me rowed over the loch
And we pulled the skiff up
Up over the bladder
Wrack of the high tide
And climbed the Soor Duik ladder.

Ben Narnain is as good
A shape as any Ben
And I liked Ben Narnain
And half-cousin Brigit.
Remember she was only half
A cousin and not het.
These words play us both
About that time yet.

All this is far too
Innocently said.
I write this down to get her
Somewhere between the words.
You yourself can contribute
Somewhere between the words
If it does you any good.
I know what I climb towards.

Is that not (Will you say?)
Is that not right, Brigit?
With your naked feet printing
The oystercatching sand?
Shall I come back to Scotland,
My ear seeking the sound
Of what your words on the long
Loch have put in my mind.

After the bracken the open
Bare scree and the water
Ouzel and looking down
At the long loch. It was
I suppose fine but nothing
Now as the wind blows
Across the edge of Narnain
And the Soor Duik burn flows.

IV

There are various ways to try to speak
And this is one. Cousin Brigit,
Sit steady. Keep us trim
And I will pull us out over
The early morning firth between

[40]

Kilkreggan and Greenock. I'll put my blades
Easily with all my sleight into
My home waters not to distort
The surface from its natural sound.

Behind your head, where I can see,
The sleeping warrior lies along
The Arran hills. Steady, Brigit,
If you would ride the clinkered skiff
And see the little whirlpools scooped
Into their quick life and go
Sailing away astern. O help
To keep me headed into the fair
And loud forest of high derricks
And welding lights blue in the sun.

Whoever you are you are; keep
Us trimmed and easy as we go
Gliding at each stroke through
The oily shipbuilding approaches.
We are here to listen. We are here
To hear the town in the disguise
My memory puts on it. Brigit
Is with me. Her I know. I put
Her in between the lines to love
And be alive in particulars.

Brigit, dear broken-song-tongued bag,
I'll not be jilted again. I see
You younger now this morning, urged
Towards me as I put my back
Into the oars and as I lean
Towards you feathering the dripping blades,
I think almost you are more mine

Than his who was before. Remember
Your name is Brigit Mooney, kin
To Malcolm in his slowly moving
Ultramarine cell of ice.

Brigit, take me with you and who
Ever it is who reads himself into
Our presence here in this doubtful
Curious gesture. Come, step over
The gunwale. I think, it seems we're here
On the dirty pebbles of my home
Town Greenock where somewhere Burns' Mary
Sleeps and John Galt's ghosts go
Still in the annals of their parish

Worksheets (unpublished poems), *c.* 1970

[From Dark Dialogues]

How they spoke, the make
Shift father and mother
Here between the poor
Shift of words or

Her shy were willing ways
Towards legend turned
Into a great bull
That the sky learned.

The man I pretend
To think I am walked
Listening in the dark
Talking to who he liked.

I hope I do not write
Only for those few
Others like myself
Poets maimed for the job.

I had to choose this way
This branks, this clamp, this iron
Impediment to keep the tongue
On its toes so to speak.

Worksheets (*Malcolm Mooney's Land*), Folder A,
c. 1958

[Son, or Who You Are]

Son, or who you are, knocking
With your word at the late door
What have you come back to say?
And hush and don't let your clever
Word knock too loud. You'll wake
More than a poetry boy can chew.
With your forefinger fish the key
Up from my side of the door
And turn the old lock easily
And do not wake your mother, though
It is not likely the way time
Whispers and waves across us all.

Worksheets (unpublished poems), *c*. 1974

[What's the News?]

What's the news, my bold
Retreater from the wars?
Play it on your fife
And rest your stump a bit.
You are the fork and knife
That ate the storm and strife.

Play your fife and I
Will bring you chitterlins.
He comes under the lamp
And I will make the words.
Settle your tender stump
Out of the night's damp.

Elizabeth, move the pot
Over nearer the fire.
Rob Kerr (at least a part
of him) has come back.
He's back to his own airt.
Bring that flannel shirt.

Hurry, Elizabeth, and bring
Maggie and Sheila out.
Old Maggie knows him well.
Tell Shaun and make him bring
His father's varnished fiddle.
Rob Kerr's come over the hill.

I'll pull the little cork.
And Shaun, fiddle easy.
Young Sheila, swing him gently
As the night goes, the night
Humming from the sea.
Rob Kerr's come home to stay.

Worksheets (*Malcolm Mooney's Land*), Folder A, *c.* 1968

The Bridge

Ah yes, you've caught me sitting alone
So early up this morning crossing
My bridges before I'll ever come
To those particular bridges. Never,
In fact, will those bridges flying
Ahead of me like carrots of wrath
Be stepped out on by me. Other
Swaying spans I'll find myself on
Before I know it, a personal dream
Yang tse kiang growling under
Me as I hesitate and look over
The yellow roar to wonder if ever
That slant-eyed bosom will take me in.

Worksheets (unpublished poems), *c.* 1970

[I Write as I Speak]

I write as I speak. Peculiar
Images ask me to take them in
To stay to be used. This morning
I am easily walking over
The high moor above Zennor

Ready to be killed by anything.
I walk under the lark and who
Should I see approaching over
The sour grasses but you round
The carn across the red ground.

Hello. You are a new one.
Do you see me saying that?
So they approached, two people
With faces they believed in having,
To stand together and say something.

Zennor Hill is a hill I can
Take or leave. But this morning
Under the endearing lark
It is a bit different because
I am by Art changing its ways.

So we approached too near
To hear or see each Zennor other.
He is nodding back trying to mean
Something I might have been.

Worksheets (unpublished poems), 14 May 1972

[Here Behind the Alphabet]

Hello, then, you at the front, yes you
With the puzzled blinkers. If you like
I'll make arrangements for you to sit
Here with me on the other side
Of language for a spell. In a way
You'll see it from the inside and as
The quick stations of silence slide
Past our ears, we might, I might
Slip you a message to take back.

Sit here with me in my bugsnug home.
There outside the window go
The flying shapes of silence always
Inviting me, the crossword lonely
Fiend to fill them in. Shouting
Is useless. It only frightens off
The necessary beasts I begin
To have an affection for. Silence
Is the boundary of every cry, the medium
Which gives the cry a shape to speak.

And what do you think tonight sitting
With me beyond all possibilities
Of communication? Your friends proceeding
In daydreams down their corridors
With cigarettes or weeping may

Wonder, for a second between lifting
A cup and putting it down, where
You are at this time, at this word
You give a meaning to. You are
With me here behind the alphabet
Silence has raked and chosen us from.

Worksheets (unpublished poems), *c.* 1974

[X]

Let us have no nonesense.
This is a real place.
Between the words the blizzard fires
Its arrows at my face.

Yet the language is having us on,
Is making cods of us.
That big wave took us two points off.
I'll pull the spokes for us.

In ice like flies in amber stands
Let us say, the cabin boy
Out of the Jeannette. Corbiere
Would speak so well about this boy.

He is frozen with every word
He spoke within Time's Gorgon cave.

Worksheets (unpublished poems), 9 August 1968

[Send Me a Note]

Send me a note. Blow me a little ladder
Of various tones and pitches against the day
And I will know how you are. Open your ear to the sly
Shapes of silence which will slide past
But, remember, they are your meat, the medium which
We have in common. Don't frighten them off.
They will allow a shape for you to speak
Within and even add to what you say
Because you chose them as you chose them. Yet
Your intention moving between that will be ready
To deviate from its nature at the last
Minute to something else. You must listen
As well as you are able when you strike
Your fingers into the breathing apertures and
Make speak the holy cylinder of sound.

Notebook 4, *c.* 1967

The Word's Name

When the word or the word's name
Falls out before us in Winter
To look at the tense fields
Or look up at the curving
Flock or rooks like iron
Filings making the sky
Another thing. Then.

I walked out on the iron
Frost of the road with almost
My dear and the low orange
Sun tinted her cheek.
It is always the right time
For everything. Although
The climate of this literary
Place freezes my balls,
I can steer her in
Under the young birch-wood
Over the crunching ground
And begin a not
Too literary conversation.

The rooks of Madron over
Hear only the rustle
Of my almost dear
And me lying below
The brittle skyline tops
Of the red dead bracken.

Here in the word's name
I am surrounded again
By that Winter place
Where my almost dear
Looked up over my shoulder
With blindly open eyes.

The talking rooks across
The white Winter put
Their noisy flying language.
Are you there are you there are you there,
My literary, almost dear?

Notebook 4, *c.* 1967

[If it is Only for You I Speak]

If it is only for you I speak
Should I specially turn into
A something vulgar else? And now

In my writing kitchen I see
You smile by the way you listen
Across the cat. If you see me

Here among my bright objects
Of sorry and happiness
On this Sunday morning

I will give you a kiss of cold
Abstract untensils. I am
At last only a ghost wanting

The ghost of unknown lips pressing
On mine. And this is not your place.

Notebook 4, *c.* 1972

Five Verses Beginning with
the Word Language

1

Language ah now you have me. Night-time tongue,
Please speak for me between the social beasts
Which quick assail me. Here I am hiding in
The jungle of mistakes of communication.

I know about jungles. I know about unkempt places
Flying toward me when I am getting ready
To pull myself together and plot the place
I speak from. I am at the jungle face

Which is my home where great and small breathers,
Experts of speaking, hang and slowly move
To say something or spring in the steaming air
Down to do the great white hunter for ever.

2

Language, but not with words, cool me down
And swipe those flies away. Why I entered
The uniform and rain-forest of my fathers
I will never know. This is a place that isn't
The place for dying in. I find myself
Wanting to ask my mother to wipe the flies
Away. But I am frightened she should see
My shot-up face here on the paddy field.

3

Language is when the speaker kills himself
In a gesture of communication and finds
Himself even then unheard. Or language is
What people hear when they are unspoken to.
It is always the wagging of an abstract
Tongue which reaches the ear. Come down again
Into the jungle metaphor with your whiskers
Alive and ready and I will see you all right.

4

Language is my very home where pygmies
Hamstring jumbo and the young pleasure monkey
Is plucked from the tree. Do not be frightened.
You are only here to be entertained and make
Something of yourself which is not true. O,
Excuse me, do you write poetry yourself?
But I know you do. Here we are among
The great cats of stature in their literary
Camouflage and all I can do is lay
My head on the paper trying to speak and then
Shift over to have my jungle-wounded head
Easy against the flank of the yellow leopard.

5

Language, I know you don't like words very much.
And yet I have to use you and be used.
I have always tried to destroy you. I hear
You now in the humming, buzzing, ticking under
Growth. Language, we have come a long way
From Ba-Ba. Reader, would you like to enter

But you have entered already, into here
Which is not really your place. There are no tusks
In (yours or mine) jumbo's graveyard. The jungle
Of words is changing and the monsoon rains
Are drenching me and drenching my uniform
Which you don't recognise. The flies are busy
Where my eyes were. Why does the language shine
Such great heat on my face. O yours truly.

Worksheets (*Implements in Their Places*), Folder A, *c.* 1974

The Conscript Goes

I

Having fallen not knowing,
By what force put down or for
What reason, the young fellow raises
His dreaming bloody head. The fox
Glove towers and the whiskered rye
He sees between just. He sees
His mother wading through the field
In a uniform of the other side.
Urine and blood speak through
The warmth of his comfortable pain.

His fingers open towards her but
He is alone, only a high
International lark sings
'Hark Hark my boy among the rye.'

II

Far at home, the home he always
Was impatient of, his mother
Is making jam in a copper pan.
His mongrel he knows well lies down
To whine and knock his tail on once
The card-table's leg. Upstairs
His young sister Jean takes
A long time to get ready
To meet her boy she isn't sure
She loves or even likes or whether
To let him do everything today.

It is my mother wading through
The broken rye and I can see
Her plain, entering my good eye.

The approaching mother bush shocks
His fading guilt. The pain has gone.
As his parochial head nestles
Into the springing field he quite
Accurately sees a high sky-trail
Dispersing slowly to the west.

IV

Father and Mother I am not here.
They stir me with a wooden spoon.
I fell. I seemed to fall. I thought
You wanted to speak to me and I turned
For a second away from what I was doing.
I am frightened of flies. Surely
You must maybe want to speak to me.

Do you think I have done something bad?
Who is right and who is wrong?
The stalks of rye rustle and
A terrible fly is on my cheek.
You know you know I am calling you.
I'll wink my good eye once for yes
And twice for no, although the lid
Is weighing a ton and not even
My pinky moves when I want it to.

V

Lark, my high bright whistler
And friend, are you still exploring
Your blue place where you see me from?
Where I am lying is any where
Near you all. Pencil and slate
Has a funny smell I can smell now
In Kelvin's School just up the road.
The girl who sat in front of me,
Her name was Janet. She liked me.

VI

Dad O Mum, I know I'm cheeky.
I will be a better boy. I'll try
Better this time. You'll see you'll see.
My new suit out of Pointers?
Is it ready safe, hanging there?
Mother I didn't like it I mean
I'll be glad to get back away.
Mum, will you put me into the kitchen
To see your bright mantel-brasses
And keep the dog from licking my neck
And keep the flies off my face.
Mother, I am not well.

Notebook 4, 25 August 1968

Slaughterhouse

Hung on the hooks the voices scream

Nightwatching here I go my rounds
Among those voices as they hang
And drip blood in the sweet drains.
I landed this job by stealth,
For free meat and the sake of my health.

Bang at the door or I'll not hear,
With calves at the back waiting their turn.
Whoever you are, it's worth a visit.
The watchman's clock is no great company
And I'll take you round for a small fee.

I've always wanted to live in a slaughter
House of my own and take my tea
Between my rounds with the clock in harness
Hung on the wall beside the stove.
The slaughter-house is a house of Love.

Notebook 4, 5 October 1969

[The Prisoner]

He opened his mouth to speak
With all the best, loved
Modulations of Man.
Out came monkeys, mews,
Whale-speech, rabies-bark,
Rebec-tunes, orgasm-cries,
Blown blades of grass between
The thumbs of boyhood, cries
Of fear blown like a key
Put up to the lips, measured
Shrills from telephones
In empty rooms, screams
Of a falling pin, gnashing
Of the teeth of a rose,
Trembling of chords stretched
Across the dark window
Of his anxious prison.

Notebook 4, 12 September 1970

[My Long Home Loch]

My long home
Loch is still
Lying between
Hills in my mind.
In memory
Reflections slow
Ly move and change
And elongate

Into gigantic
Wisps alive
In their own right.
Loch Long lies
Held still between
Hills after
My words write
On the long water.

Notebook 4, 23 March 1967

Notes

'The Ballad of Willie Peden'. Of this, Graham says, 'Prepared third ballad to follow "Baldy Bane" and "Broad Close" and to be "slower" in its speed and to be longer – this was the 9th draft of the ballad as far as it got and was written about 1952.' Signed W. S. Graham, Gurnard's Head, Cornwall.

'Surrealgraphs'. On 20 November 1976 Graham added a note to this poem stating: 'I know I know. I know I know I will not want to do anything with this. I know why. It is because it is too filled with objects and activity which could never go into verse in that way. Because I had no real edge on my imagination, I had to crowd the space with lines of remembered happenings which once moved me. There is no tension or silences. O please forgive me. It is an easy mistake to fall into. We are all human. But, of course the least human is the poetic beast which by God, I am almost becoming. W.S.G.'

'A Dream of Crete'. The following is an excerpt from a note to Robin and Sylvia Skelton that Graham wrote in his third notebook: 'Where am I going, R. & S.? Maybe you will remember that I pin things up on my wooden wall and as well as drawings I sometimes put up words not saying HOME SWEET HOME or BLESS THIS HOUSE. But phrases which might be useable or otherwise mean something to me. It so happens at the moment, my dears I have up – A DREAM OF CRETE (I feel it would be truer to spell it with a K.) which, as a title, more than charms me.' This was written in Madron on Christmas Day, 1972.
    Other later passages from a projected and never completed poem with the same title may be found in *PN Review*, Vol. 16, No. 5, in an article 'Dear Pen Pal in the Distance: A Selection of W. S. Graham's Letters', edited by Ruth Grogan. Being wholly fragmentary, they are chiefly of epistolary and biographical interest.

'[In the Street of Knives]'. In the pamphlet *Uncollected Poems of W. S. Graham* (Greville Press, 1990) there is a poem entitled 'The Street of Knives' which has the same setting. It is dated 29 April 1979.

'[From Dark Dialogues]'. On this worksheet Graham wrote: 'Early "Dark Dialogues" notes. Phrases and ideas apparent in finished version in *Malcolm Mooney's Land*, the book, I mean. W.S.G. 1–1–70.'

'Five Verses Beginning with the Word Language'. This was revised many times and the final version is titled: 'Language Ah Now You Have Me'. In 1975 Graham added a note to this particular worksheet: 'I see this as a man dying on the paddy-field in Vietnam.' On another worksheet, he states: 'I am reminded that the very beginning of this poem sprung from me trying to write about a soldier dying on the Paddy fields of Vietnam of a belly-wound and the flies at his face and wanting his mother and not knowing what he was fighting for. W.S.G.'

'The Conscript Goes' was originally titled 'The Young Fighter Dies'. Graham crossed this out of notebook four and added: 'It was an attempt at something.'

Sources

Notebook 1
Measures 31.7 × 20 cm; blue boards, lined paper. Titled and signed by W. S. Graham: *Notes On The Making of Verse*, October 1954. With an additional note (1972): 'Even for the quotes I'll miss this. WSG'. Contains ink and pencil sketches of heads and comments entered by W. S. Graham in 1972.

Notebook 2
Book: *Artificial Limbs* by F. G. Ernst, London, n.d. Measures 25 × 19 cm; brown boards. Letter on inside cover from W.S.G. to Robin Skelton, 9 October 1974, 'From Gurnard's Head Days'. Contains defaced illustrations, also ink and wash drawings and paintings.

Notebook 3
Measures 32 × 15 cm; red boards, lined paper. Titled: *Places*, Woodfield, 25 April 64. Contains notes for the volumes *Malcolm Mooney's Land* and *Implements in Their Places*, and for the poem 'Clusters Travelling Out', and a letter to Robin and Sylvia Skelton dated Christmas Day, 1972.

Notebook 4
Book: *Toward the Well-Being Of Mankind: Fifty Years of the Rockefeller Foundation* by Robert Shaplen, Doubleday, New York, 1964. Measures 31 × 23 cm; white paper on brown boards. Contains defaced text and photographs, also ink, watercolour and chalk sketches, and several glued-in worksheets and notes dated and signed 1967 to 1973.

Worksheets (*The Nightfishing*)
Folder includes ballads, TS and MS; signed and dated 1950–54.

Worksheets (*Malcolm Mooney's Land*)
Folder A contains miscellaneous worksheets, TS and MS; most signed and dated 1956–67.

Worksheets (*Implements in Their Places*)
Folder A contains miscellaneous poems, TS and MS; most signed and dated 1970–75. Folder B contains worksheets for 'Ten Shots of Mister Simpson', TS and MS; signed and dated 1969–71.

Worksheets (unpublished poems)
Folder contains twenty-nine unpublished poems and worksheets with and without notes, TS and MS; most signed and dated 1966–76.